COLOR TEST PAGE

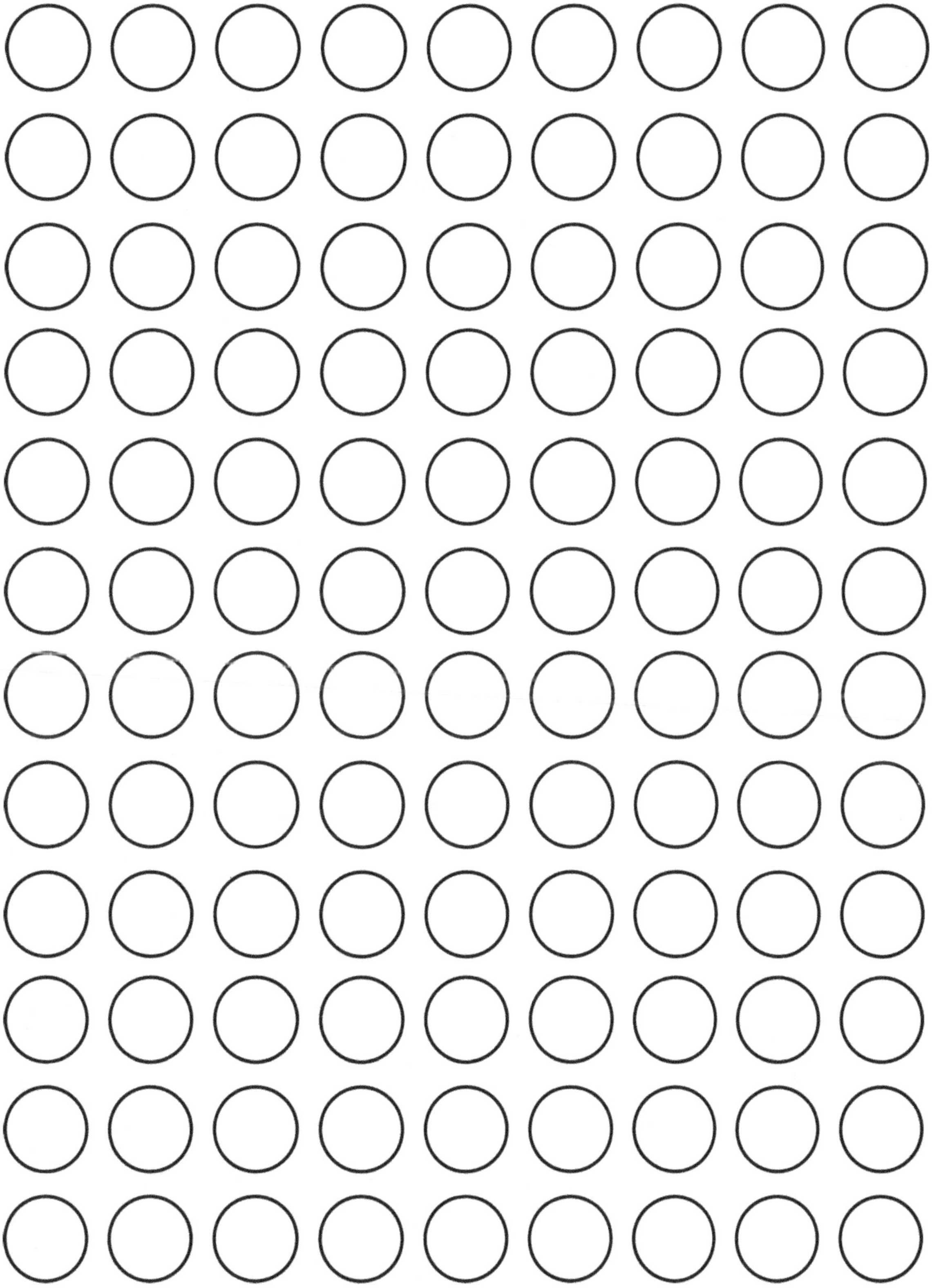

FLOWER

MANDALA PATTERNS

COLORING BOOKS FOR BEGINNERS

Vol.3

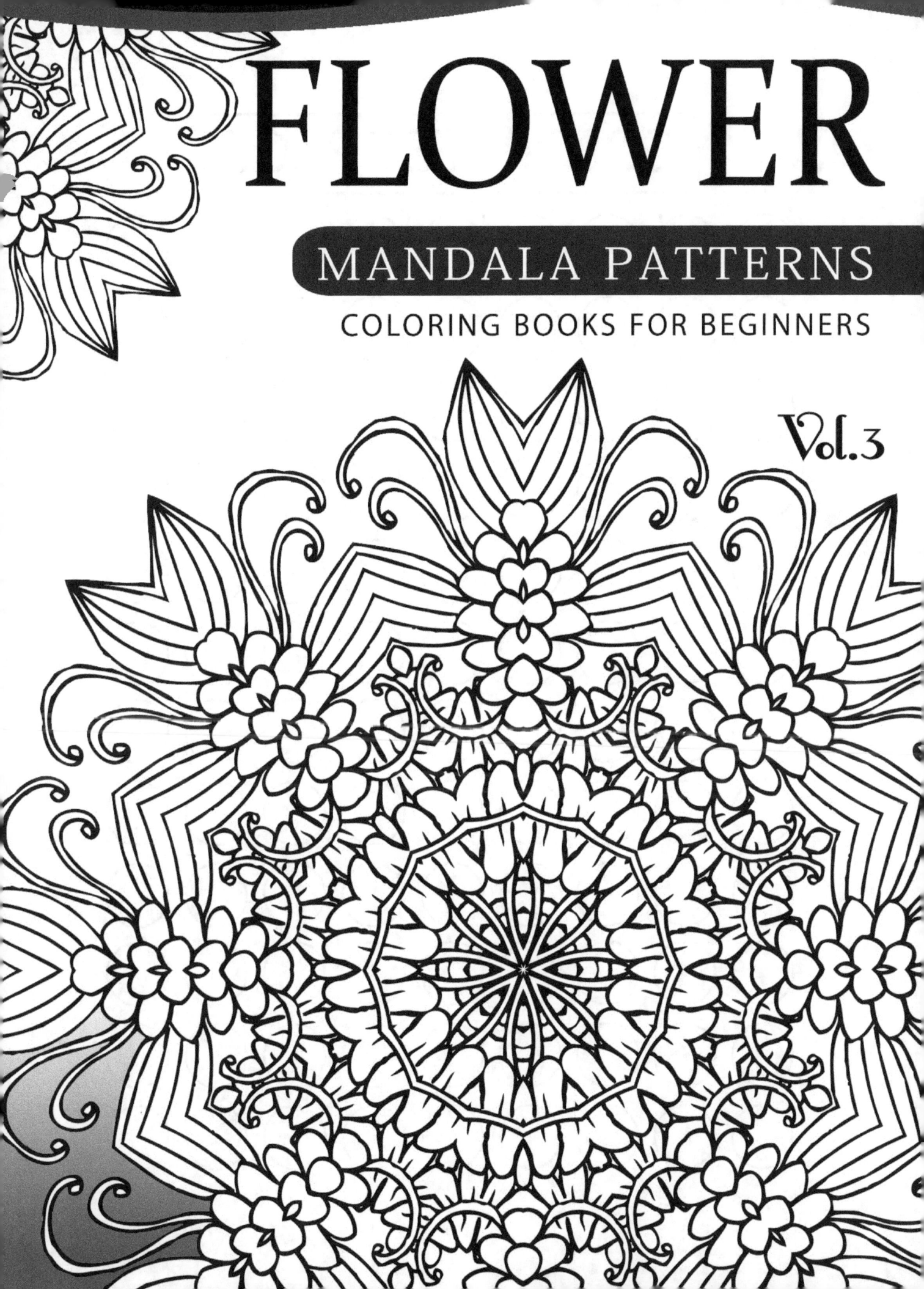

COLOR TEST PAGE

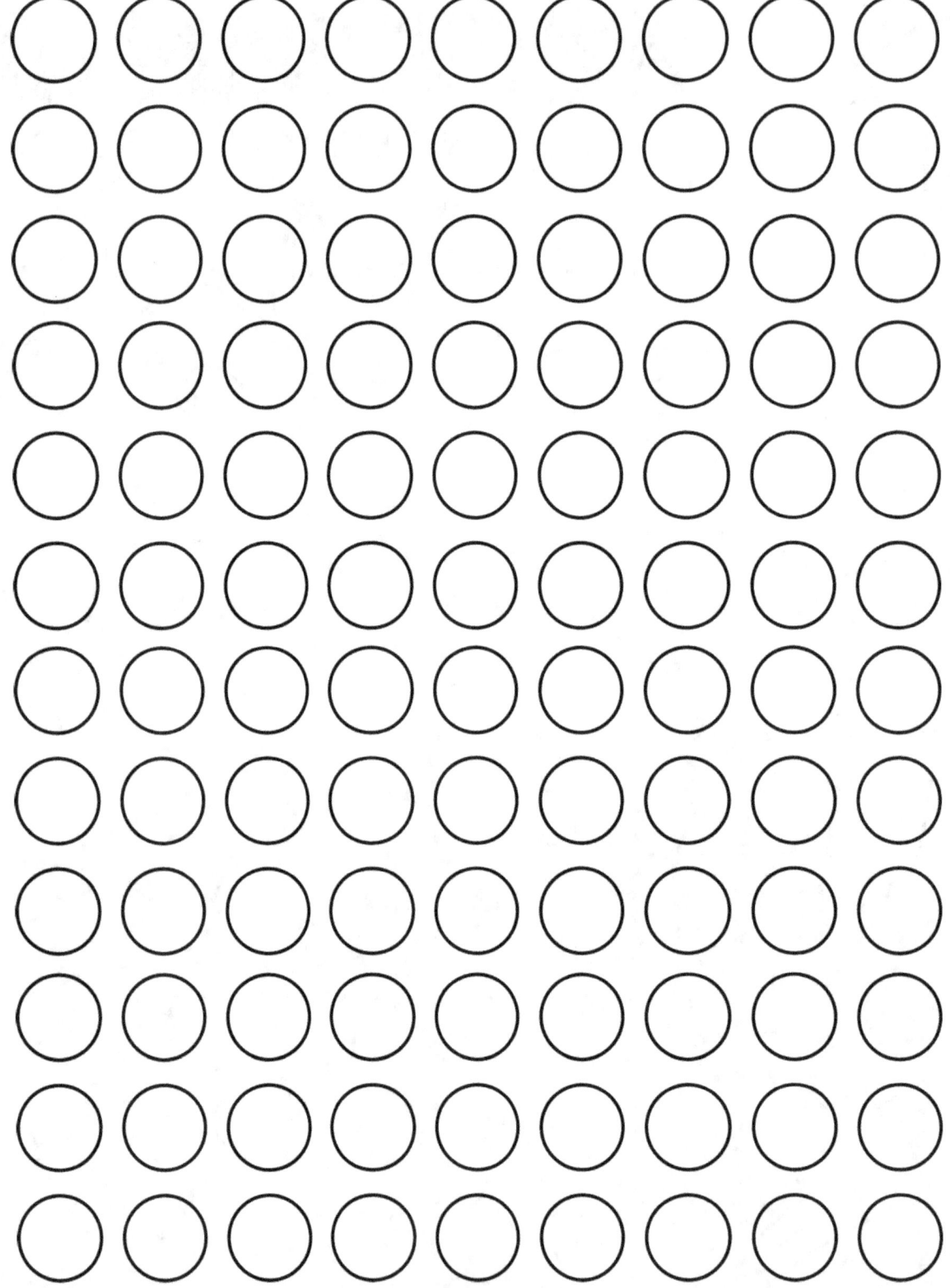

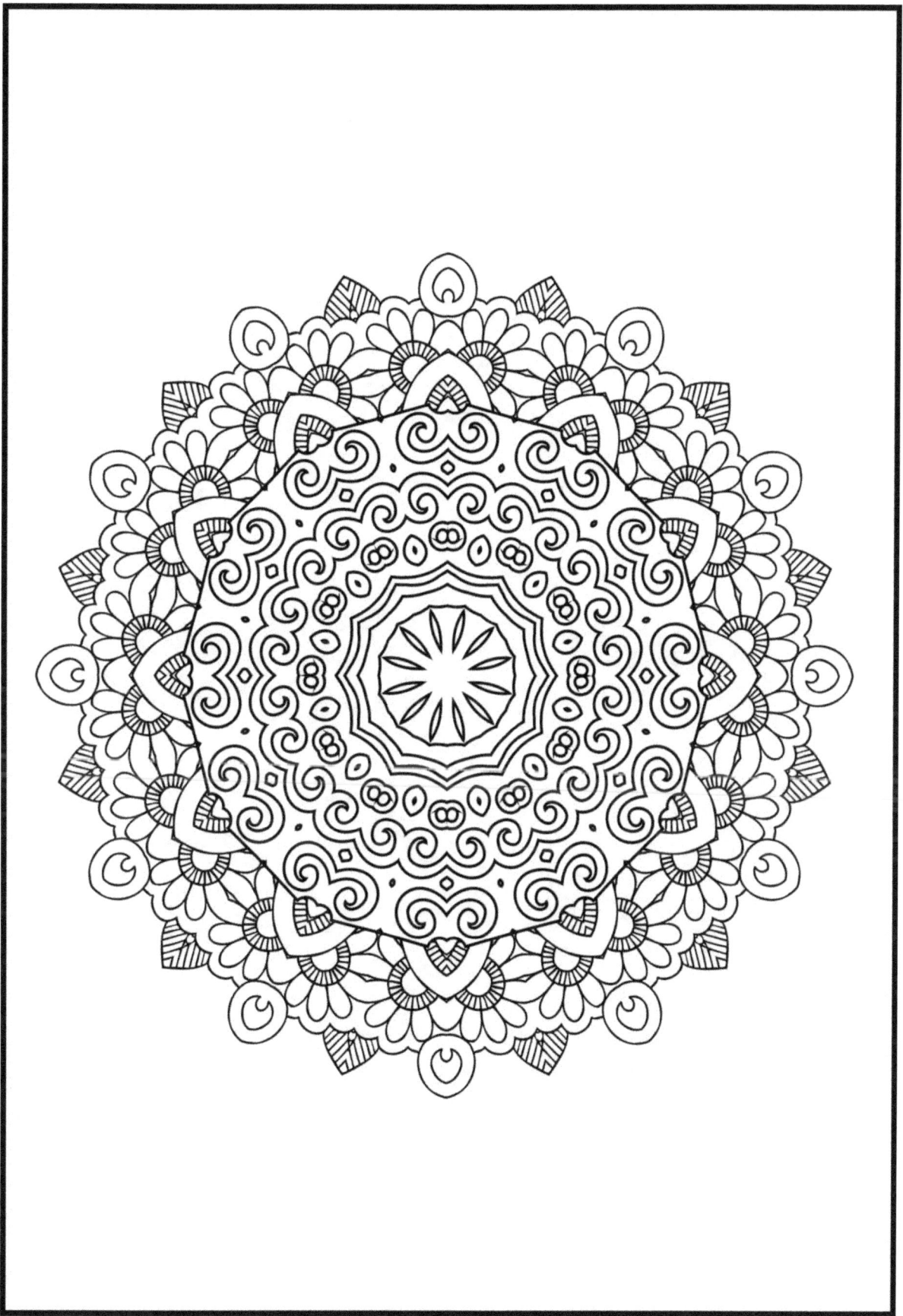

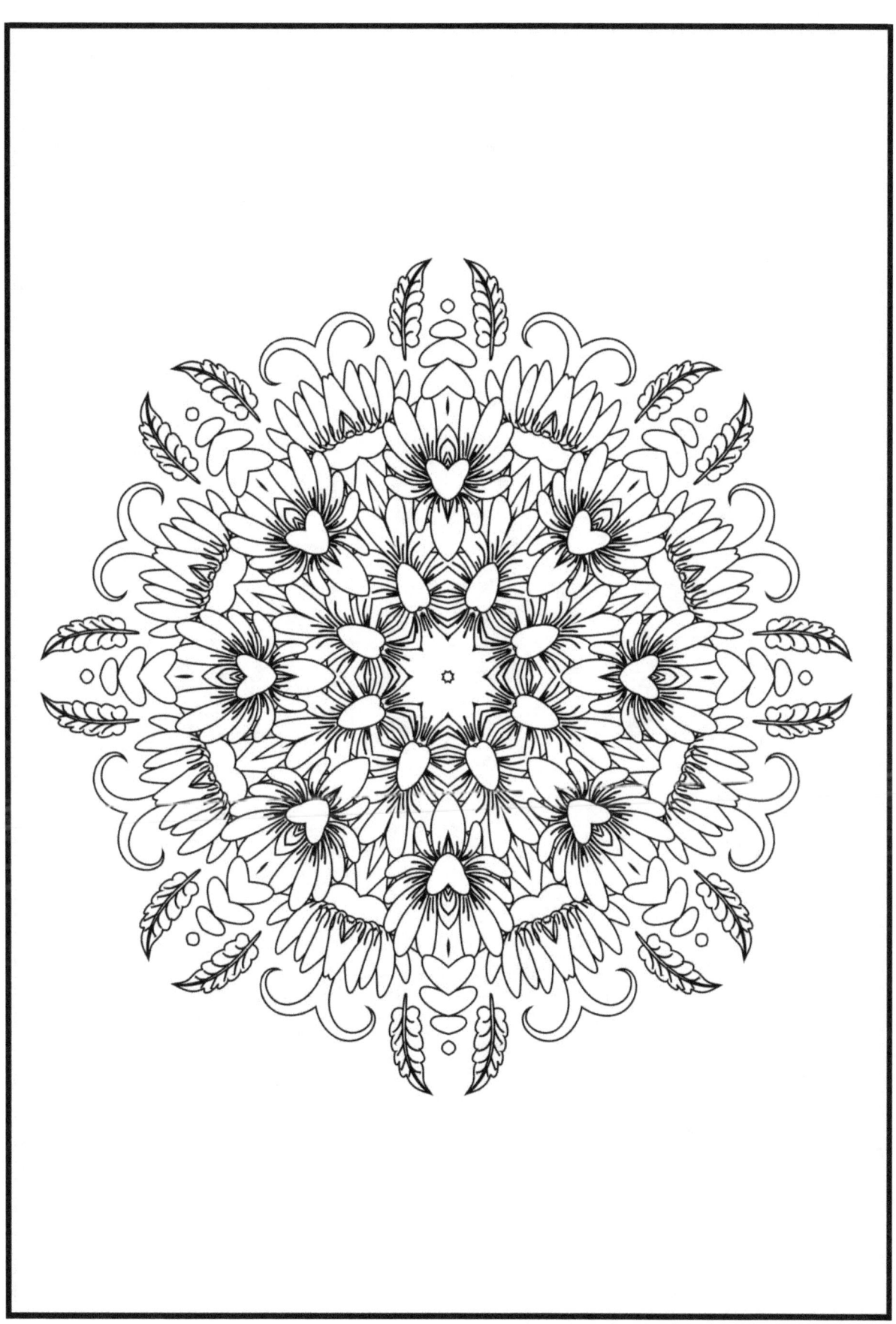

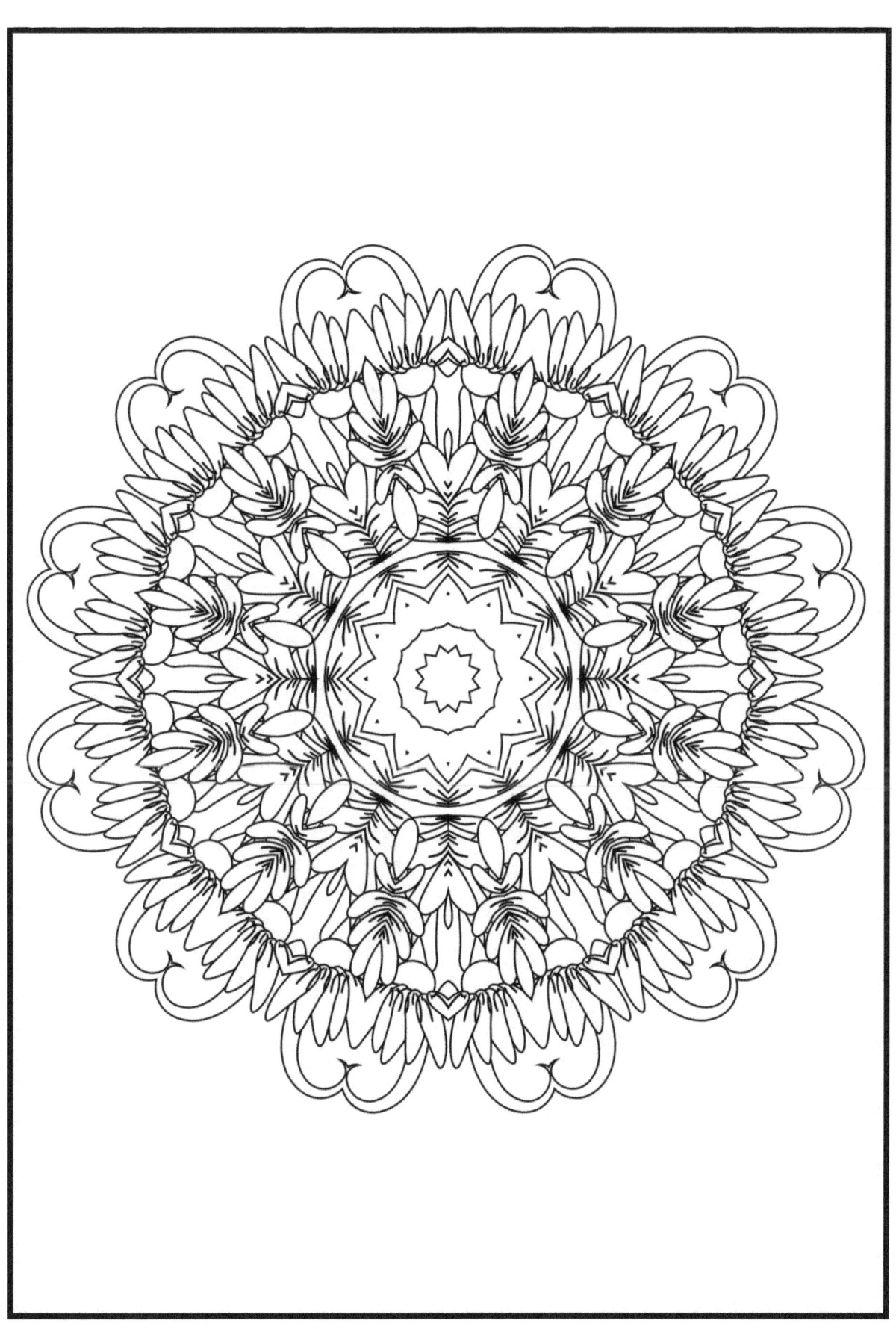

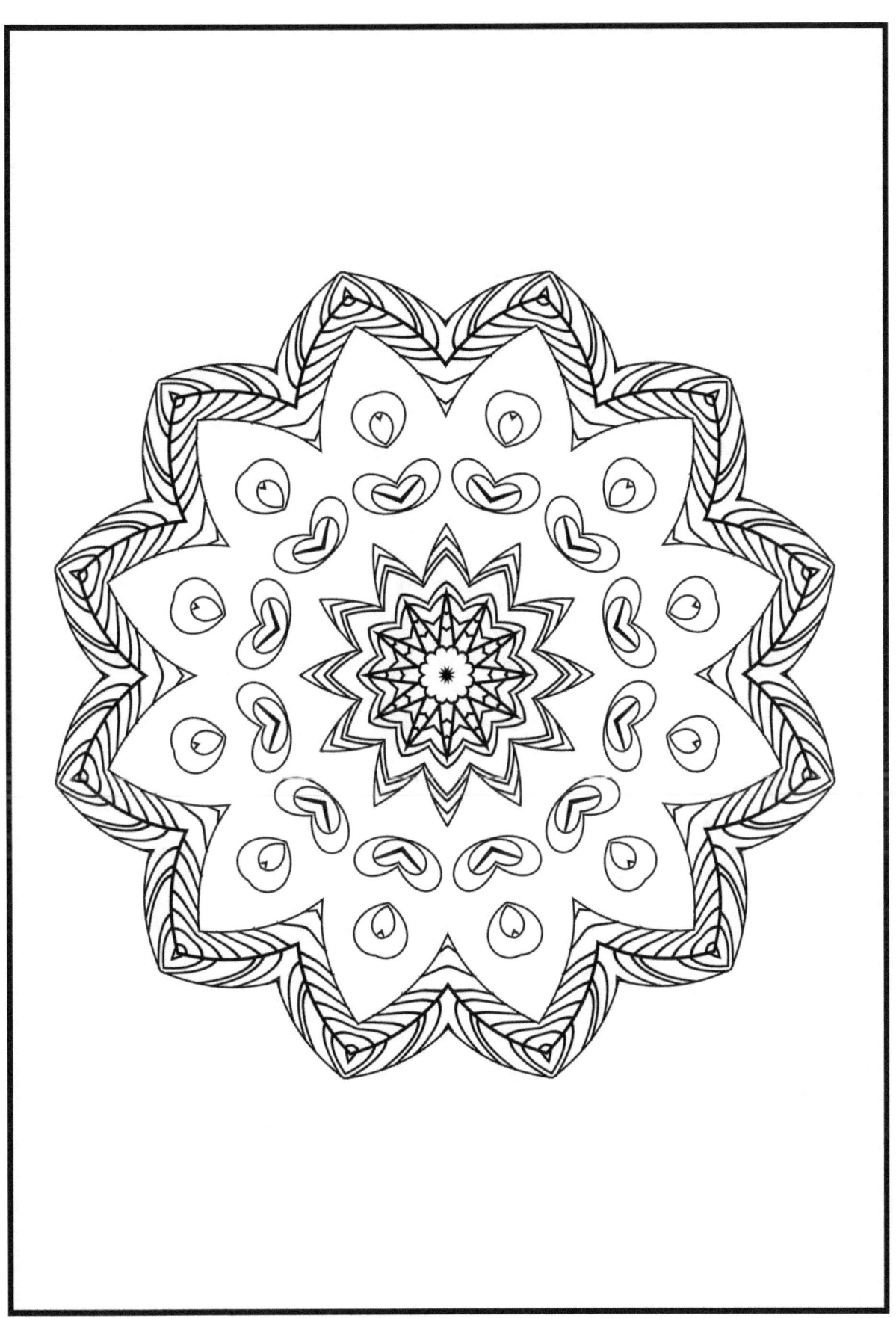

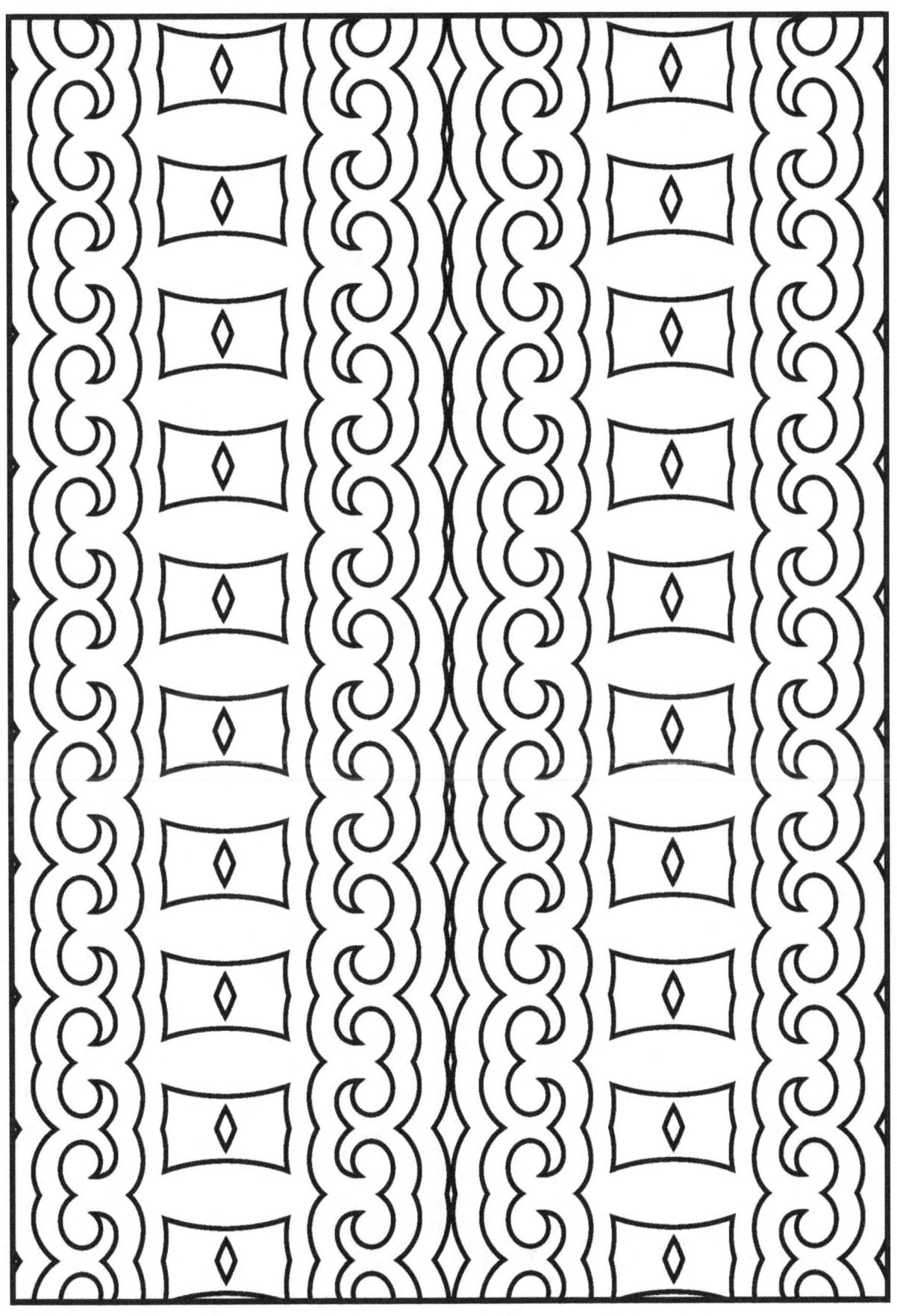

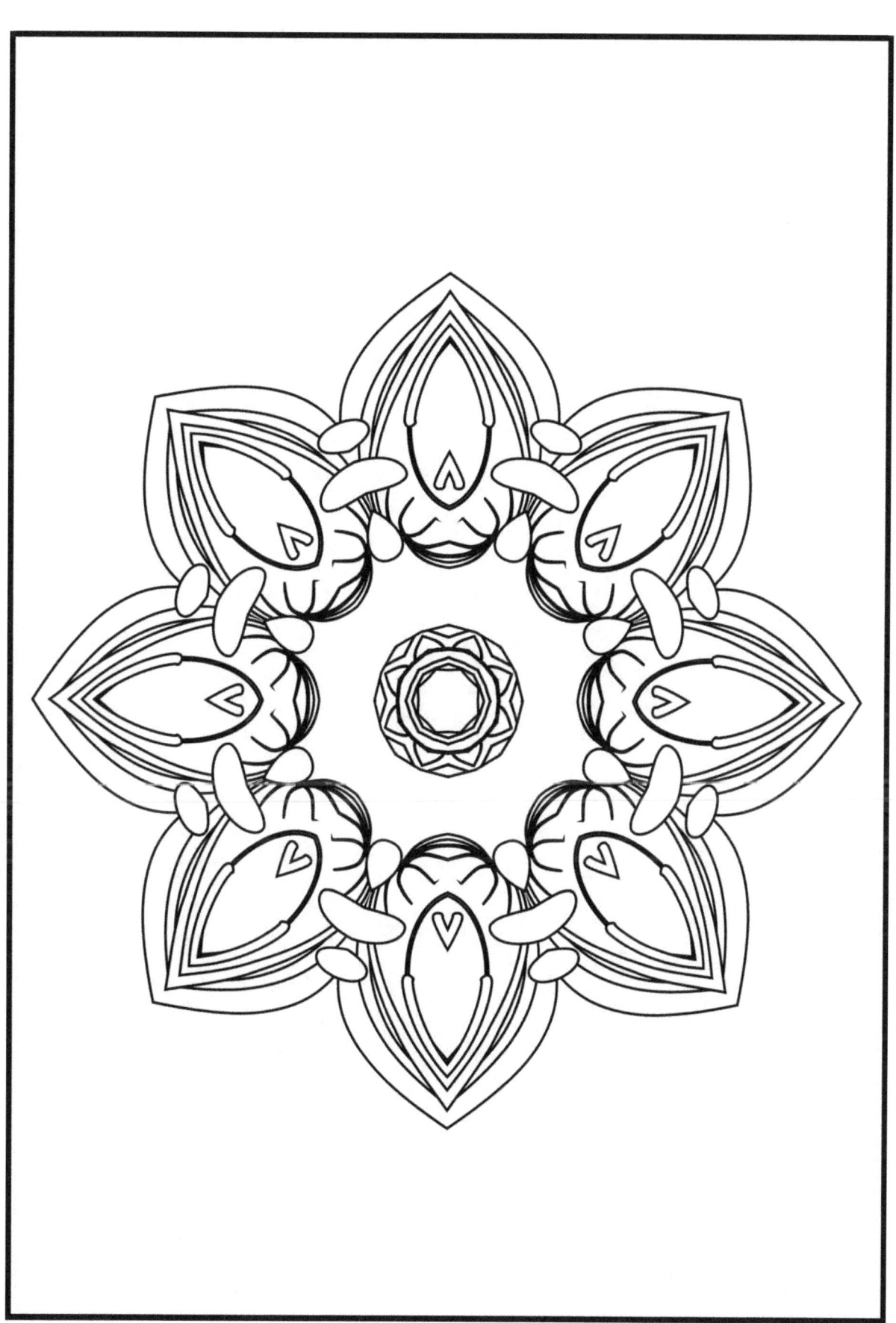

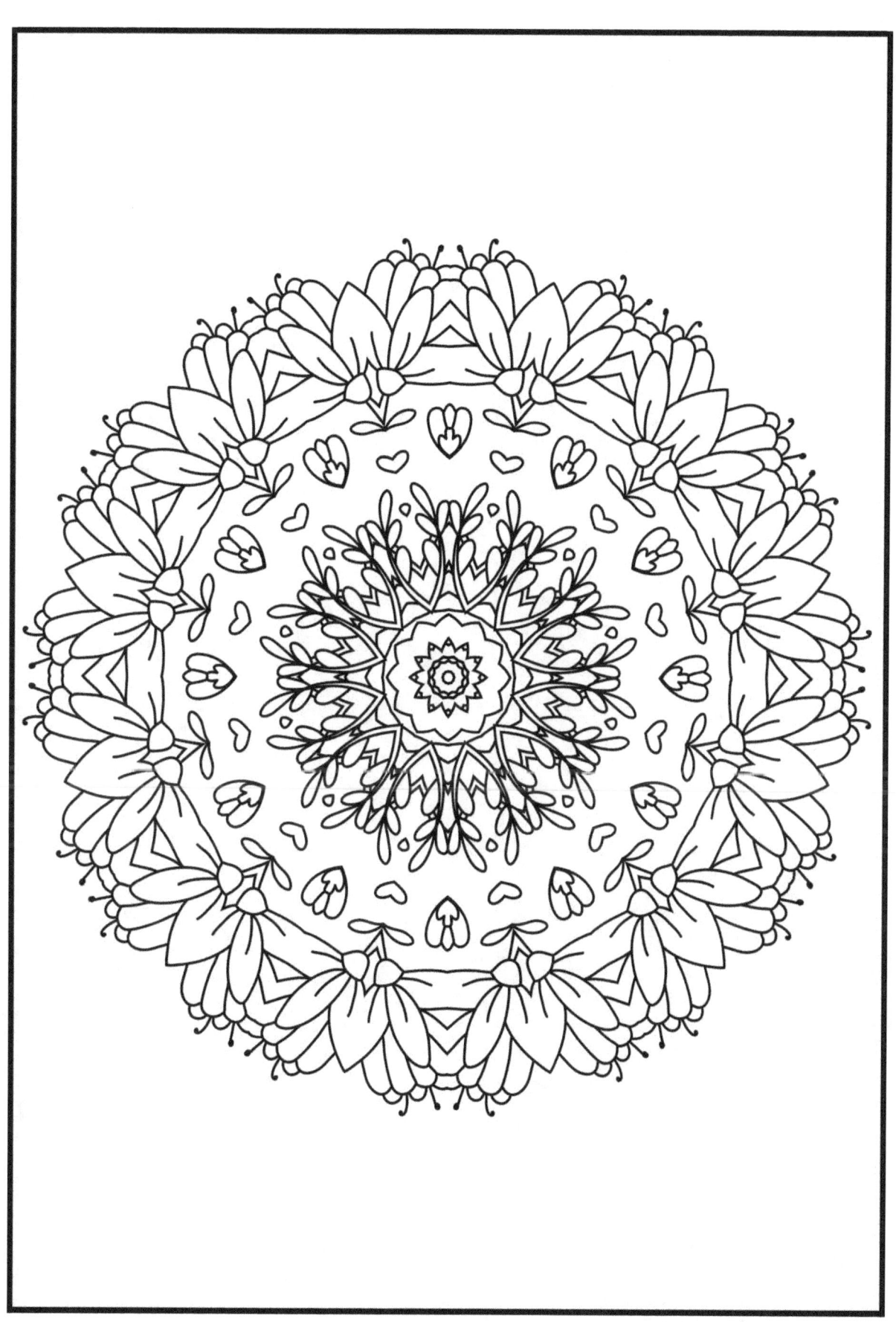

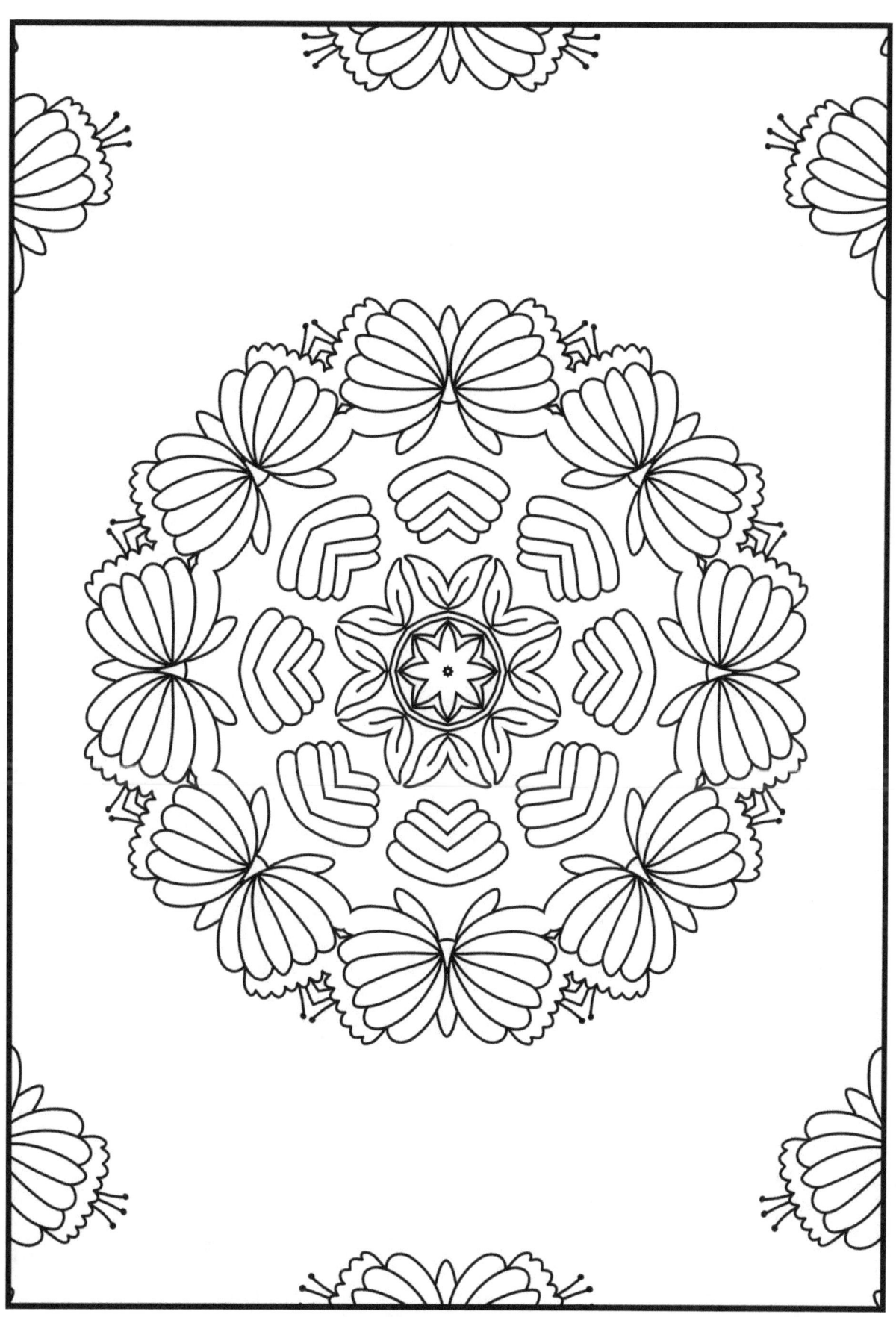

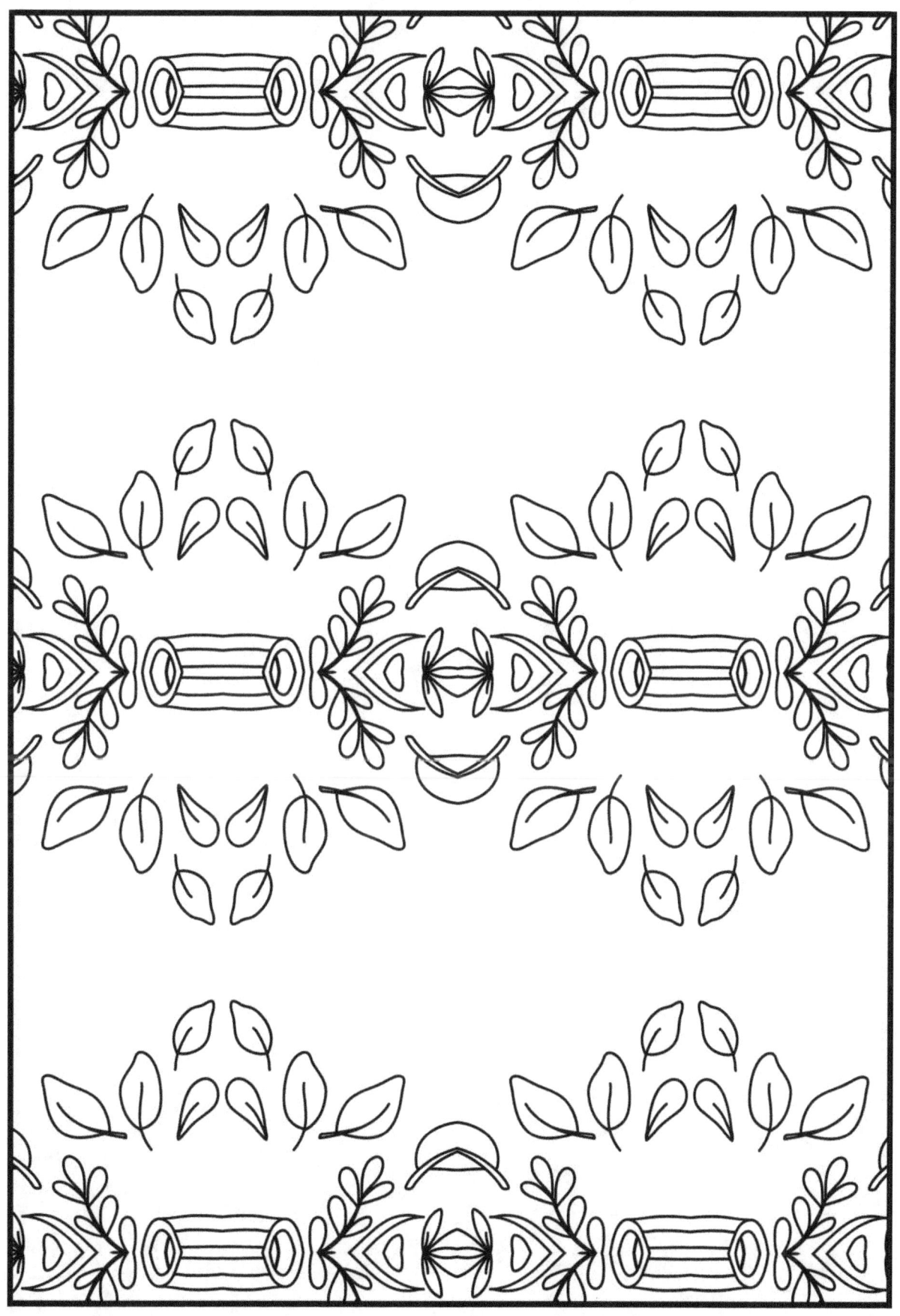

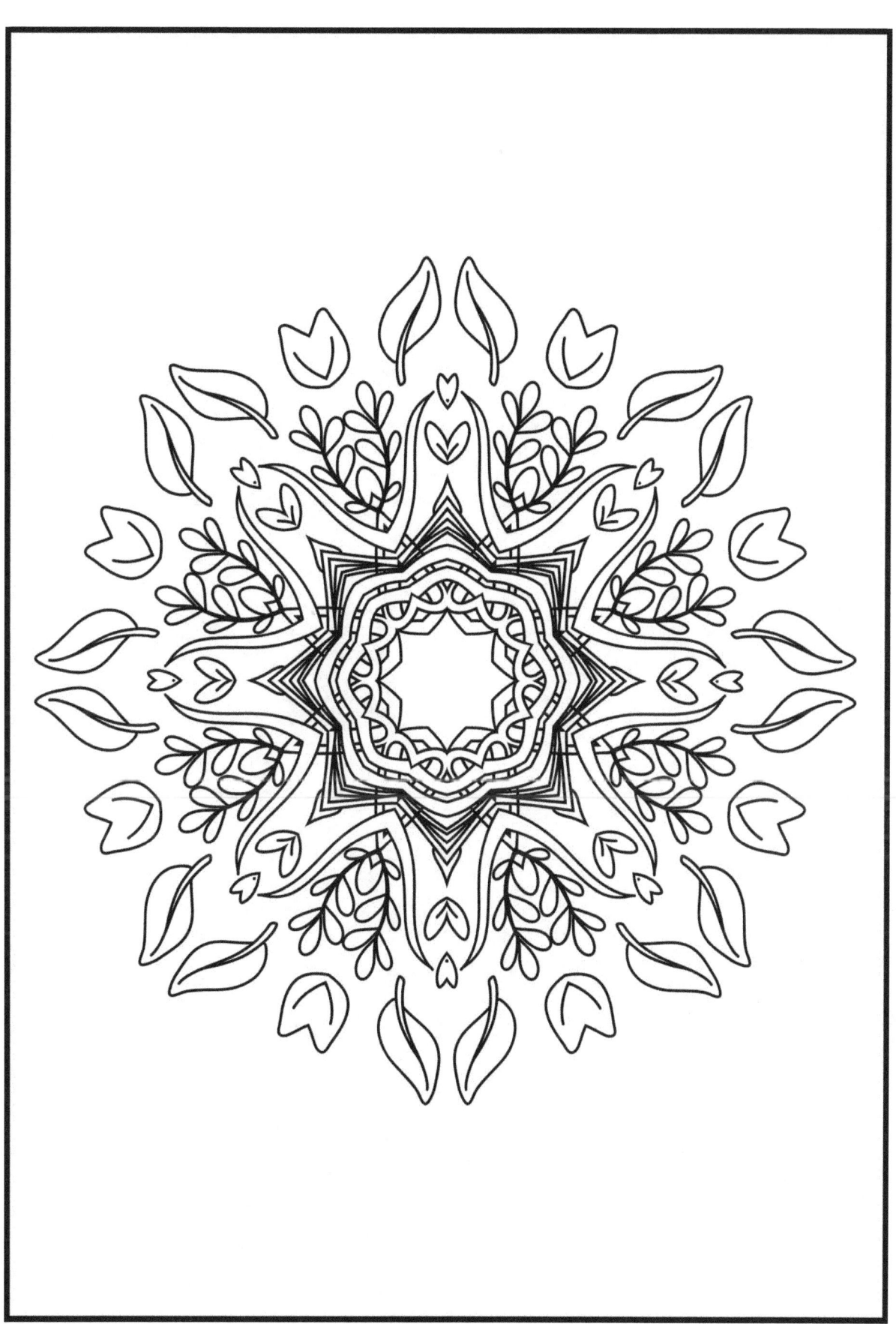

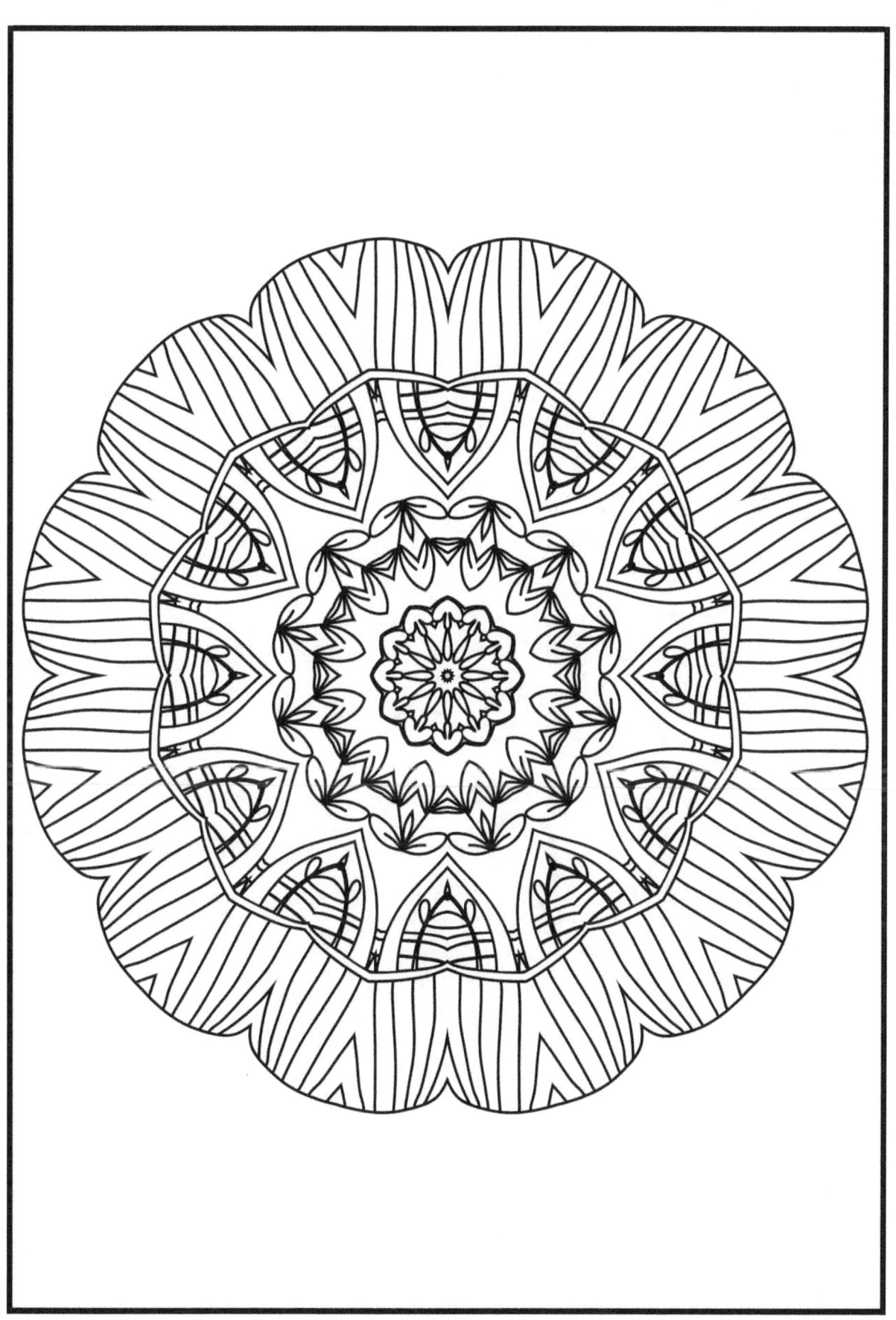

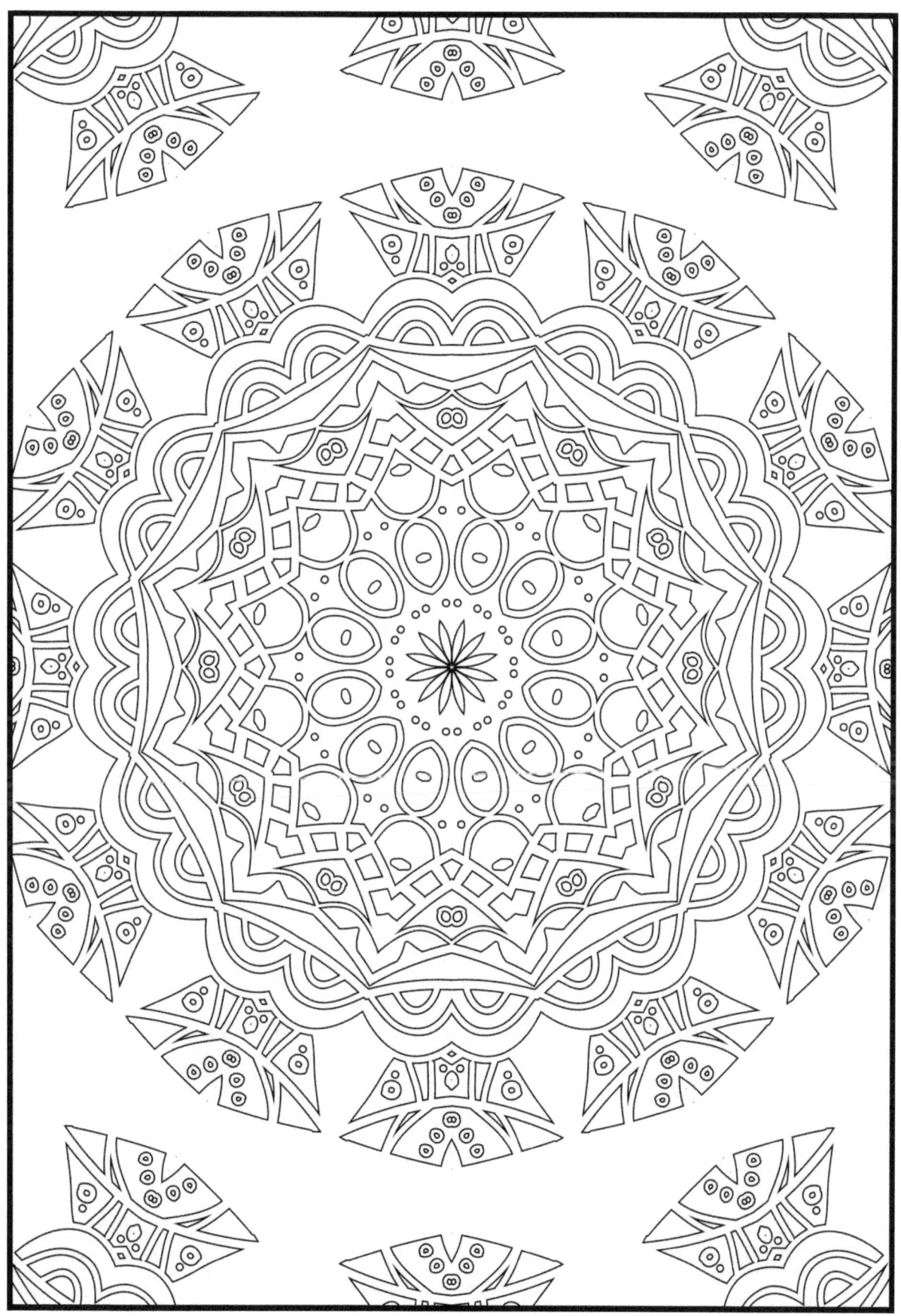

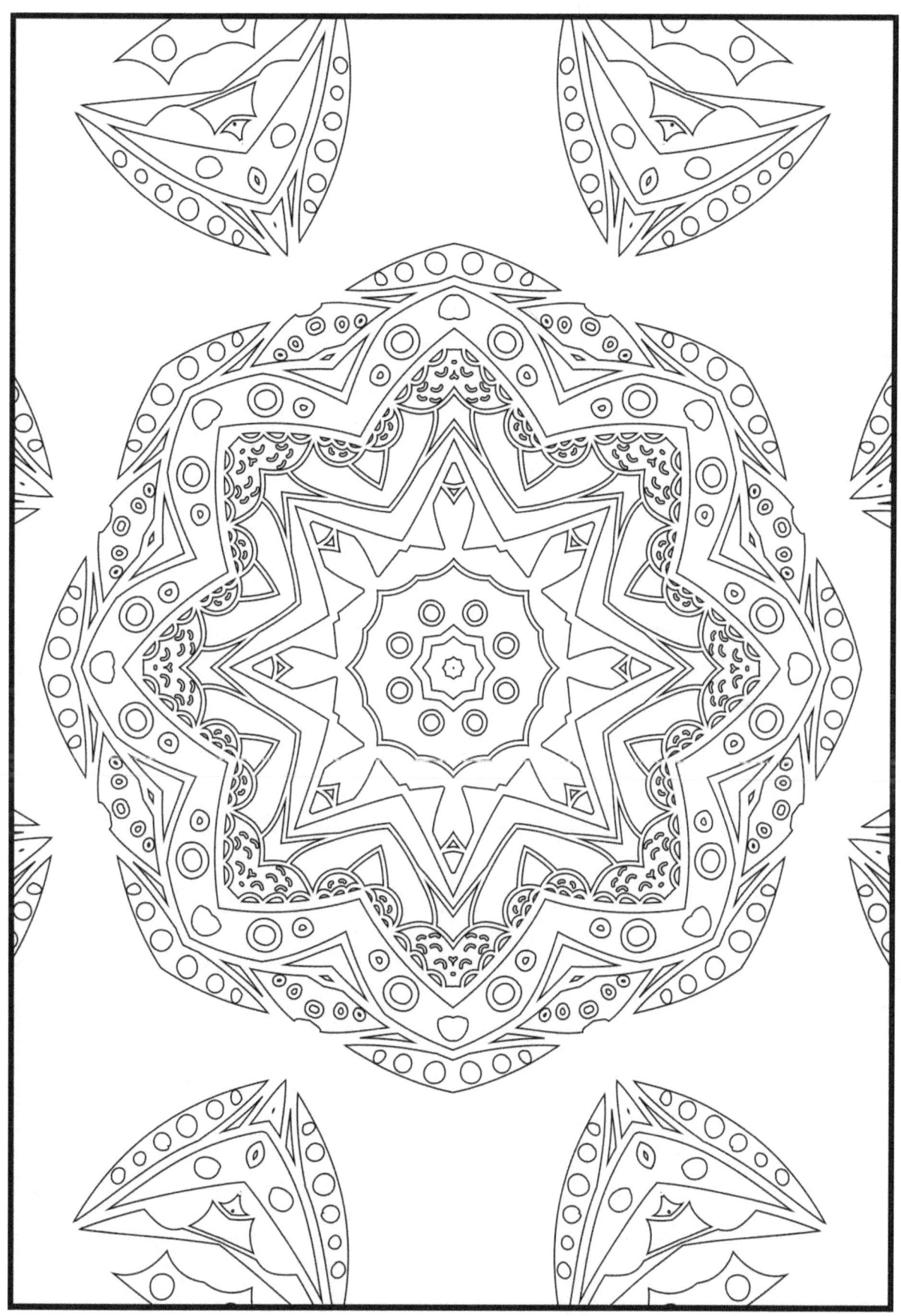

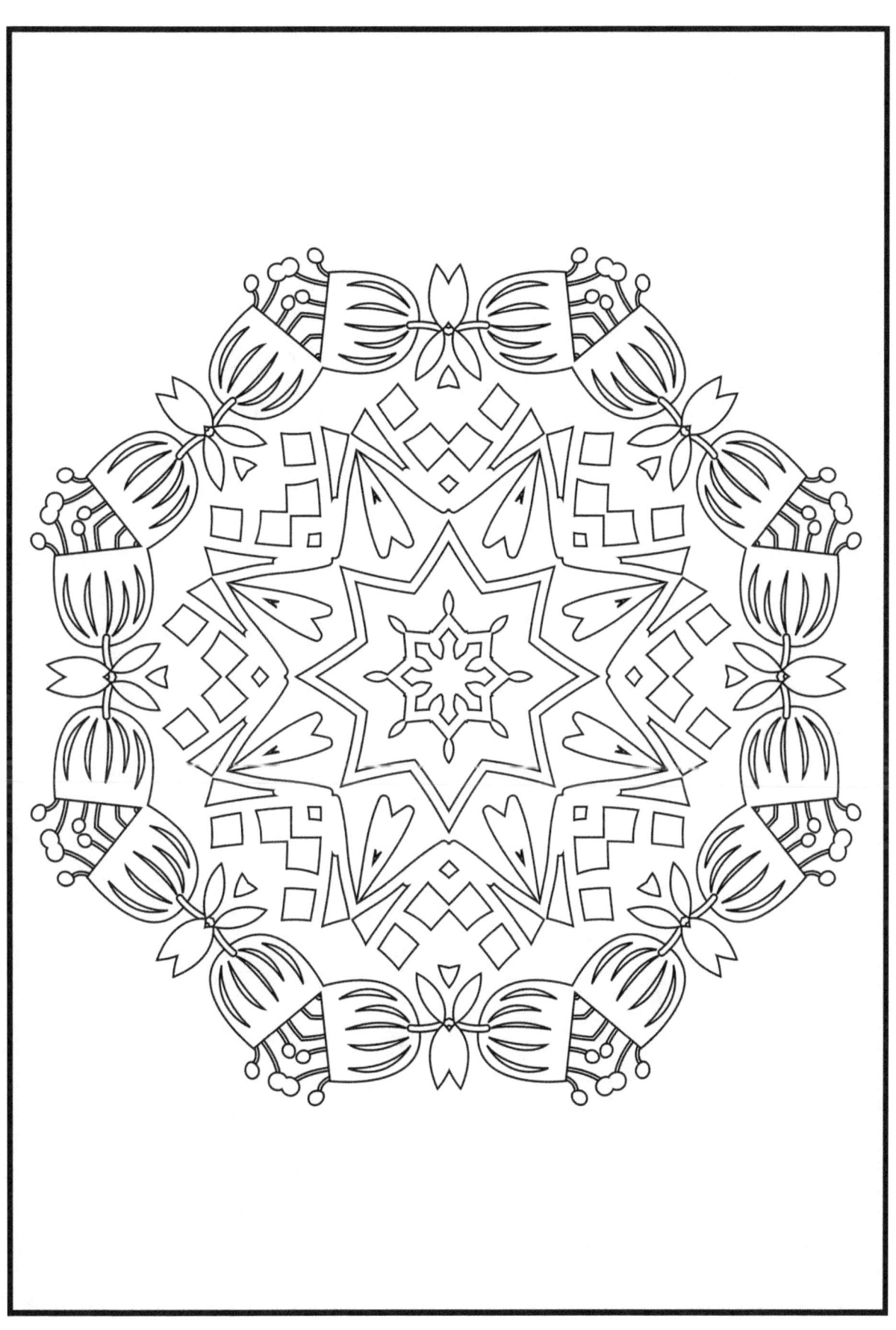

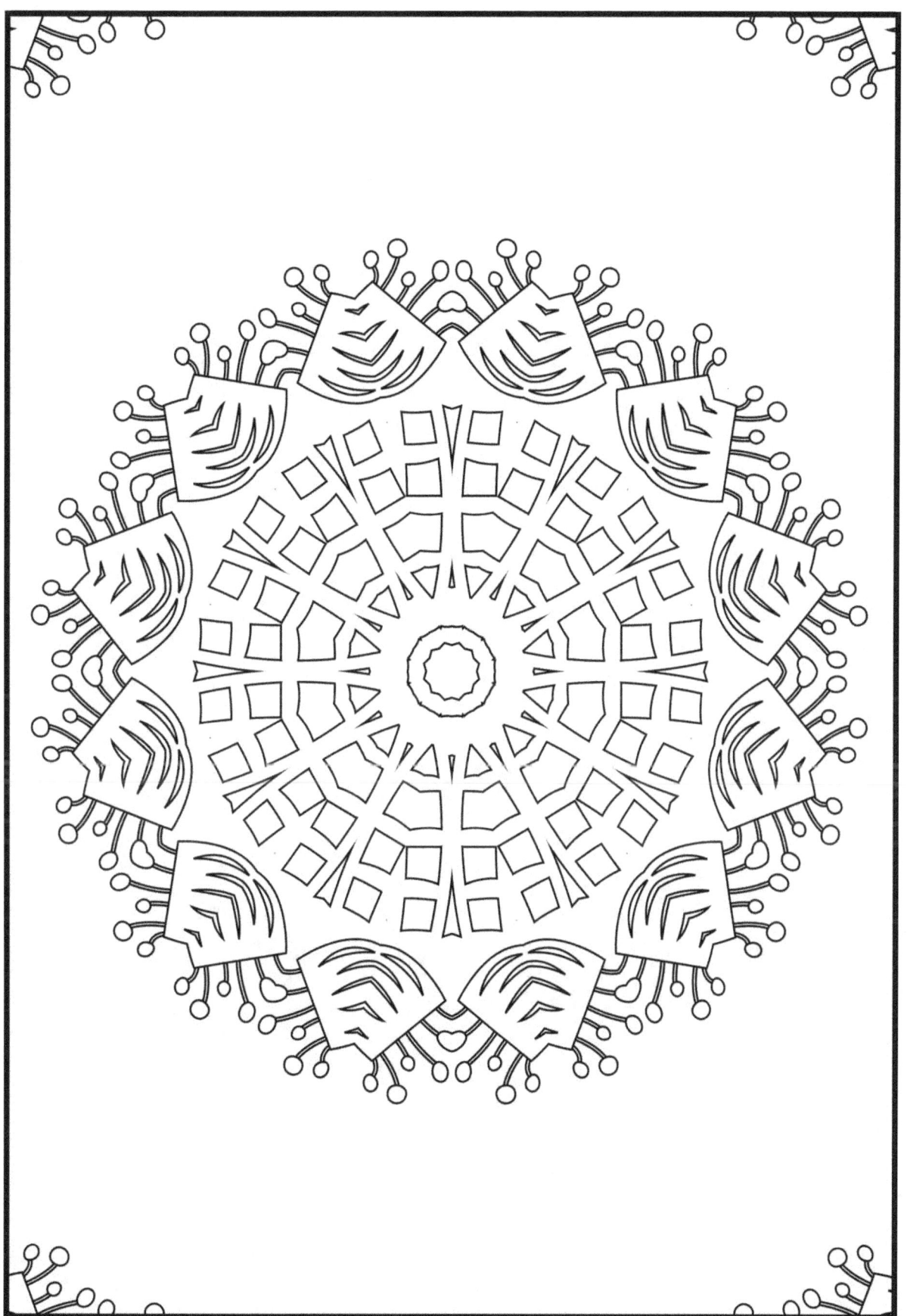

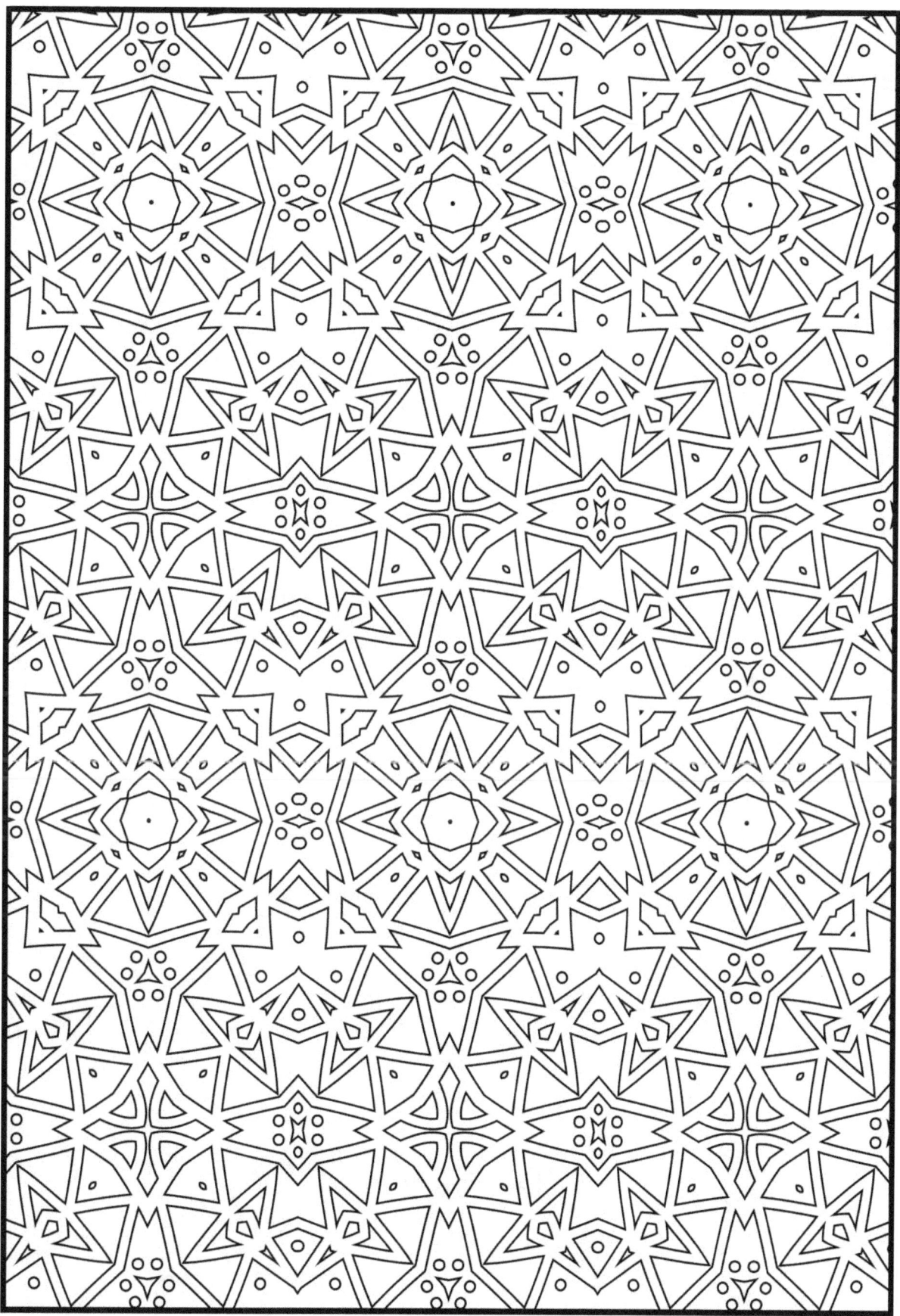

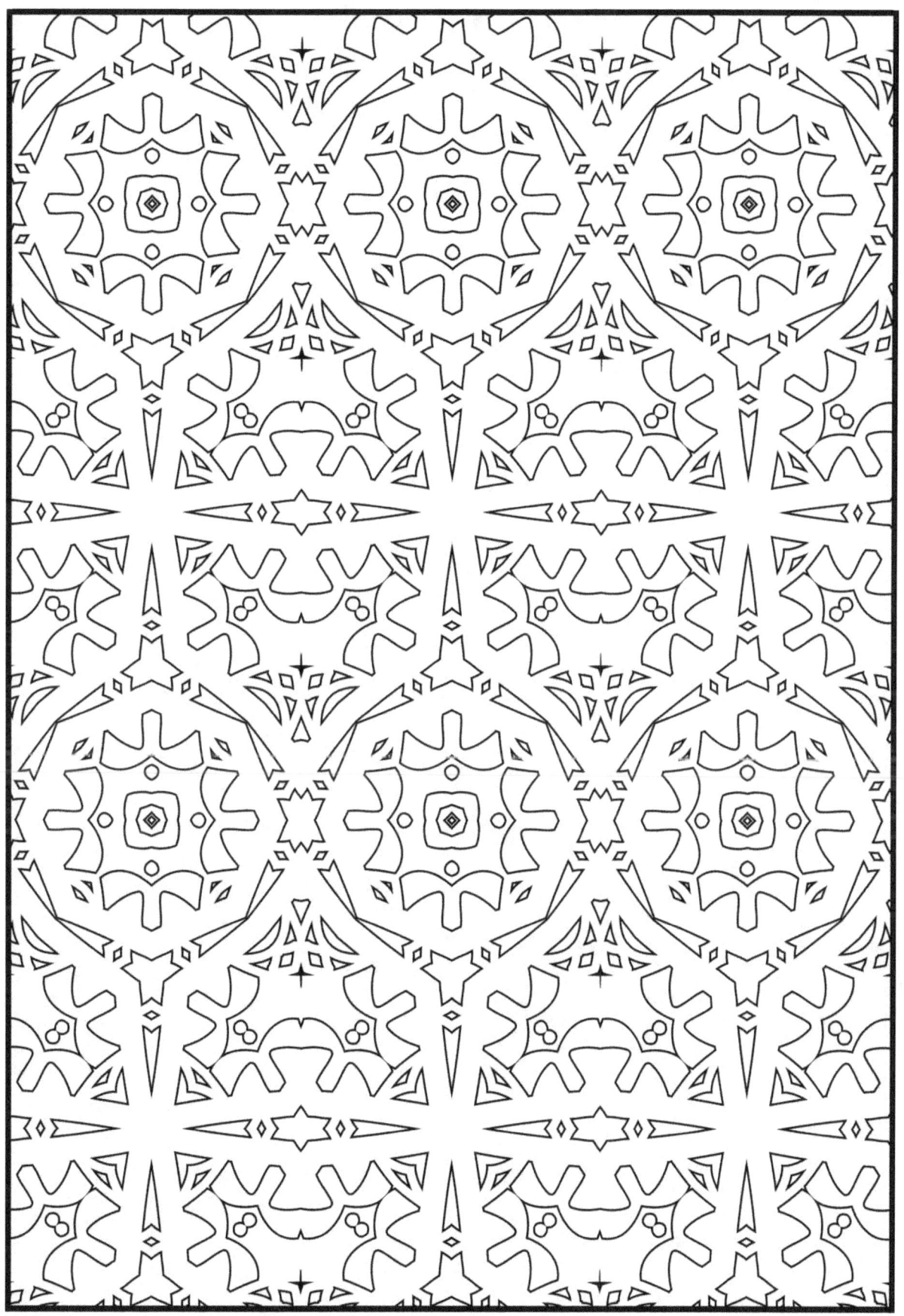

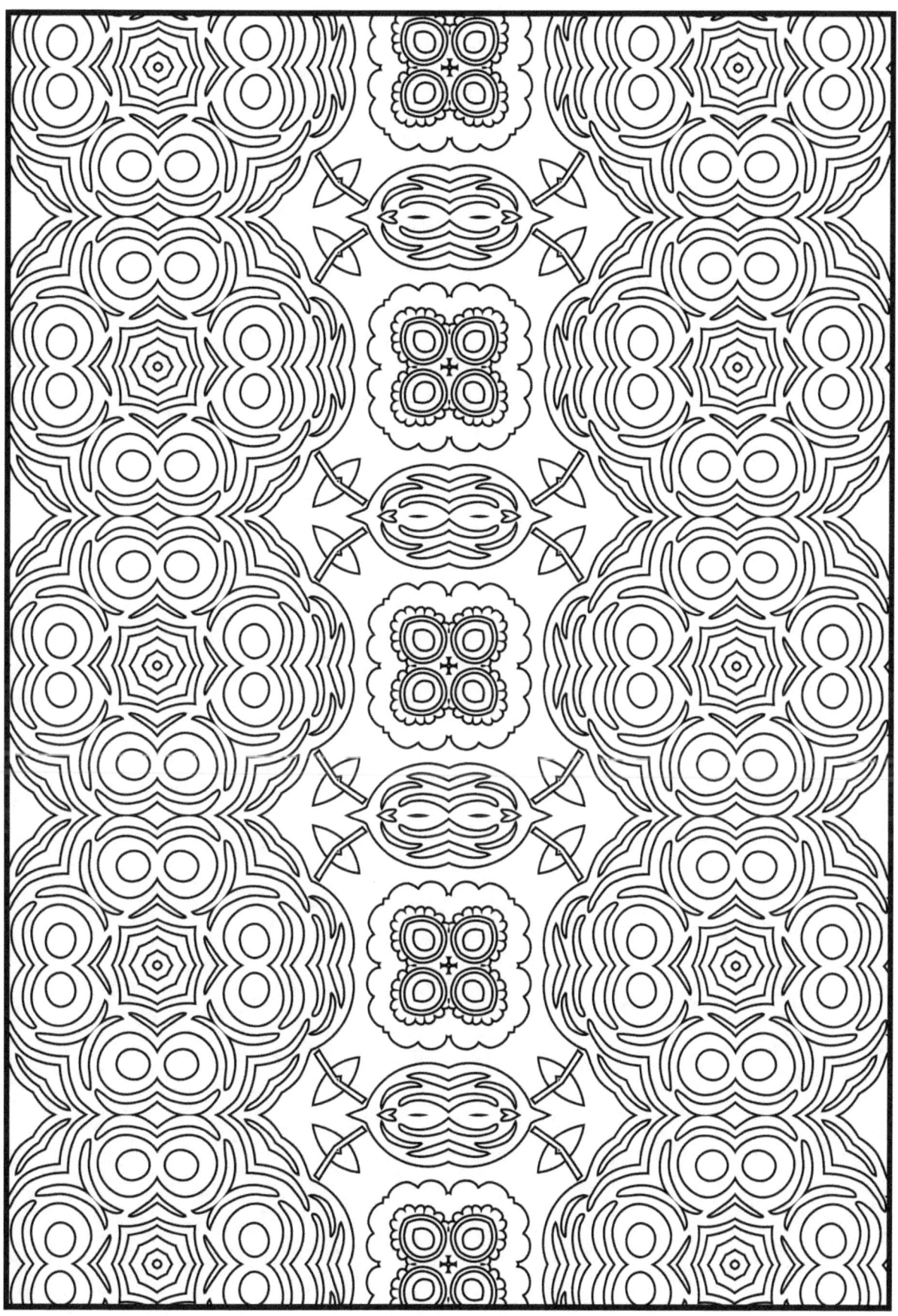

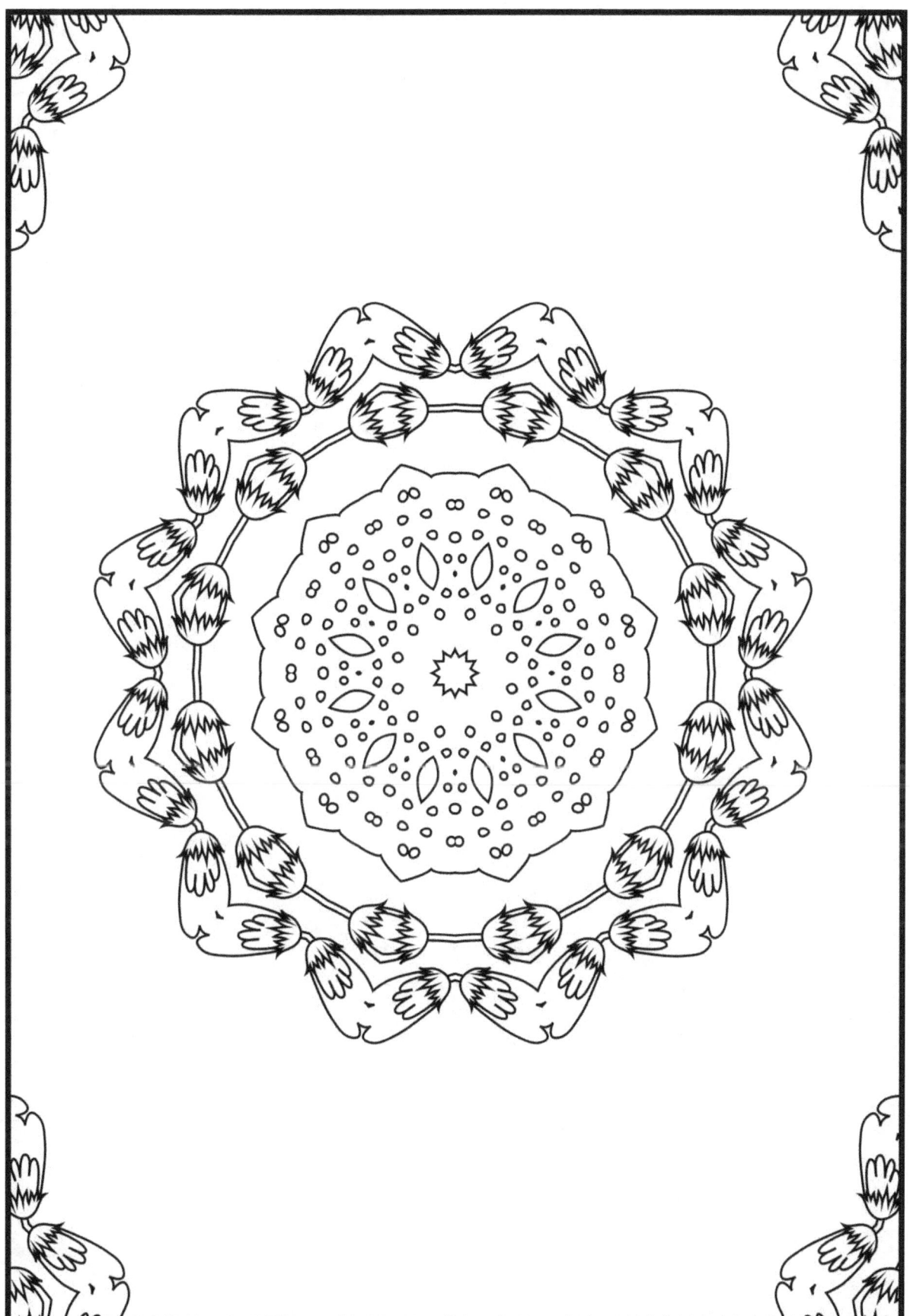

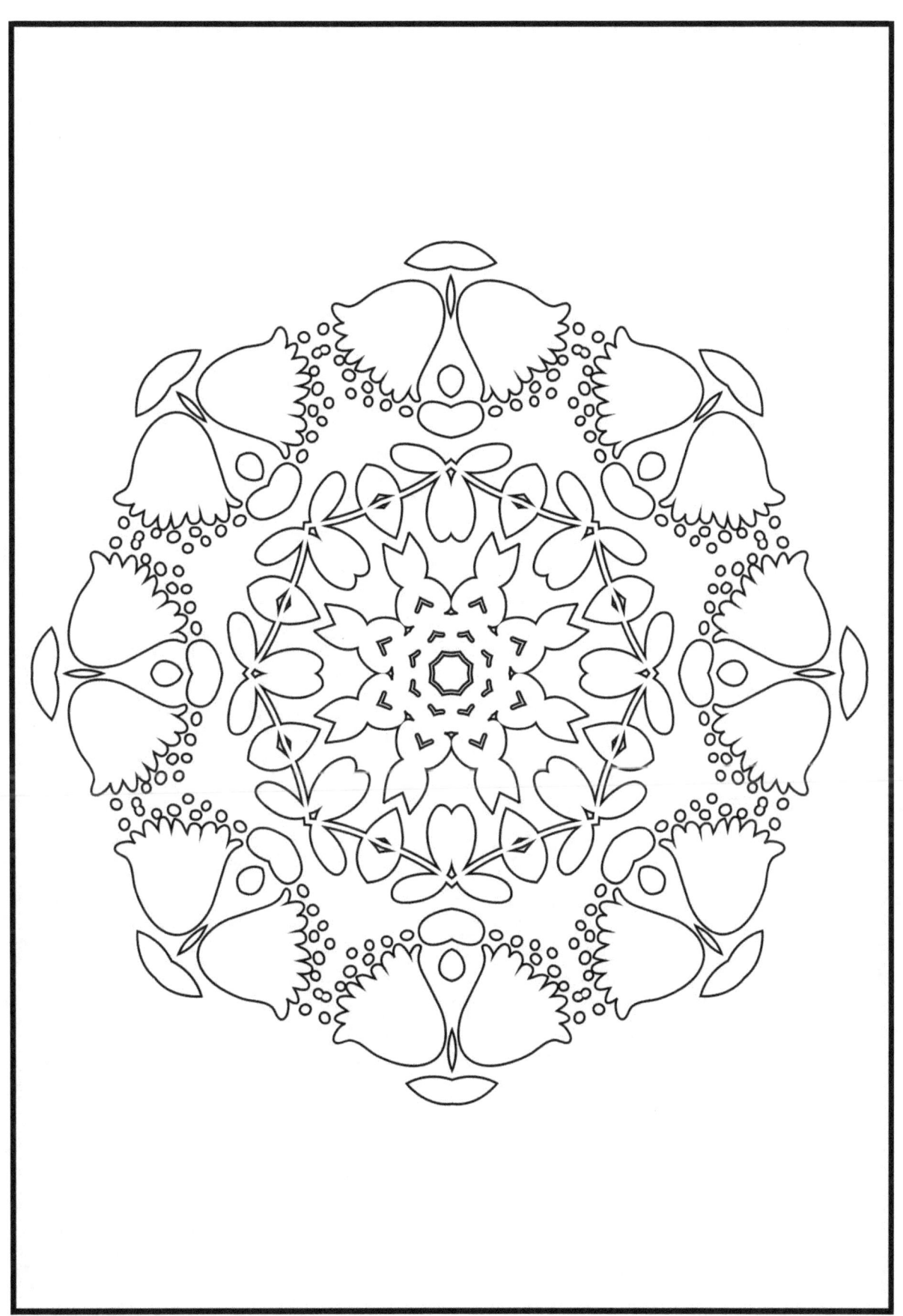

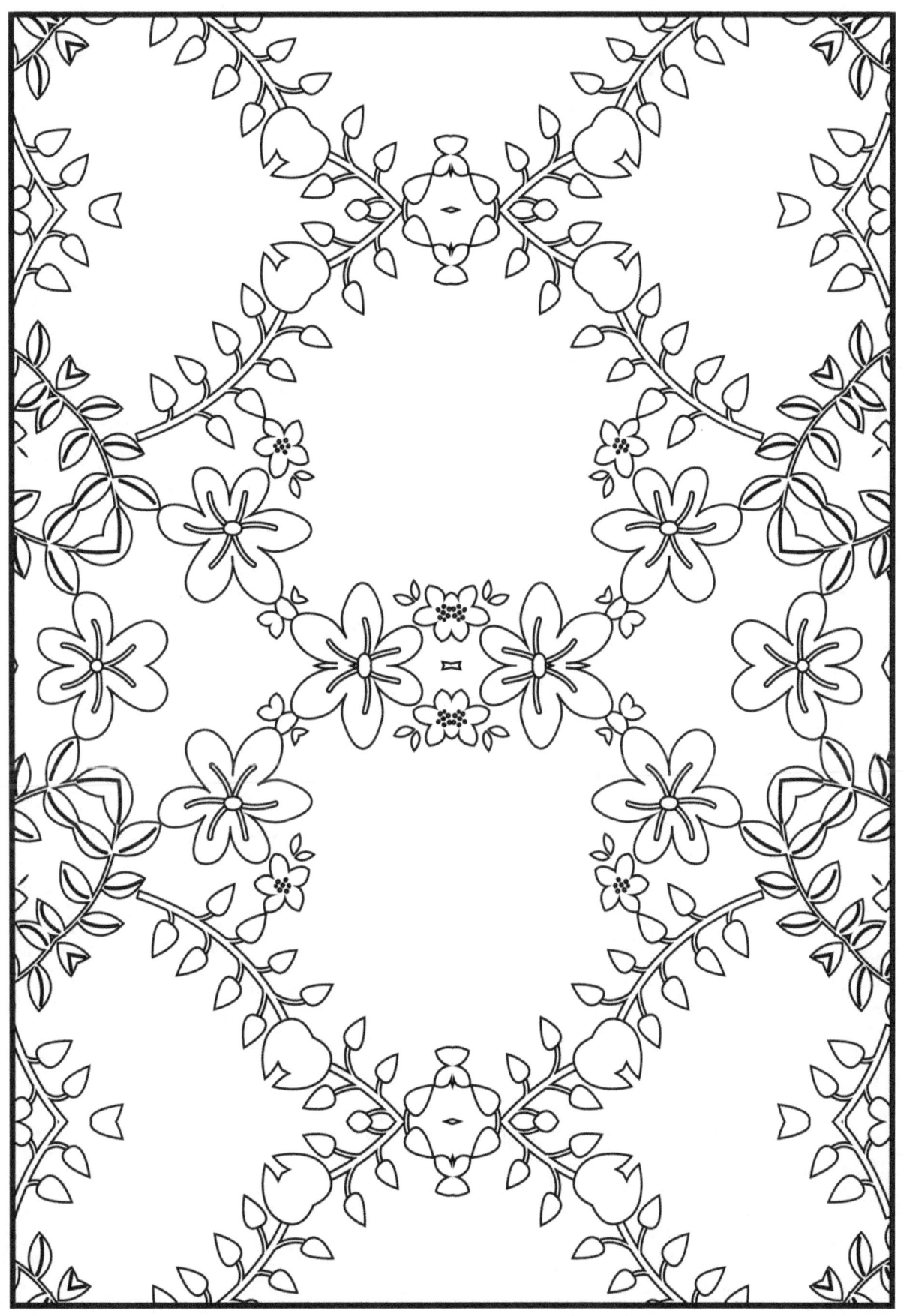

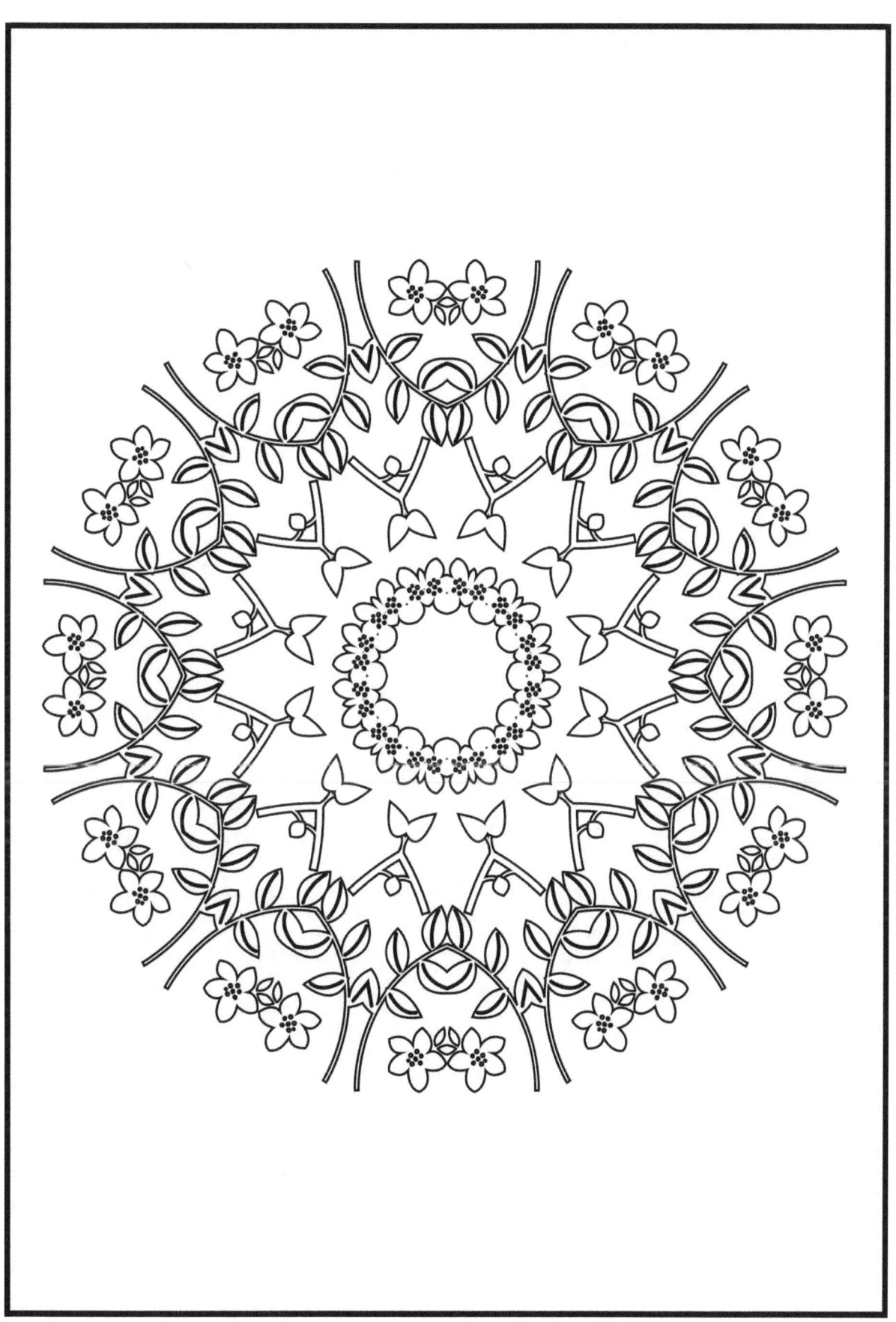

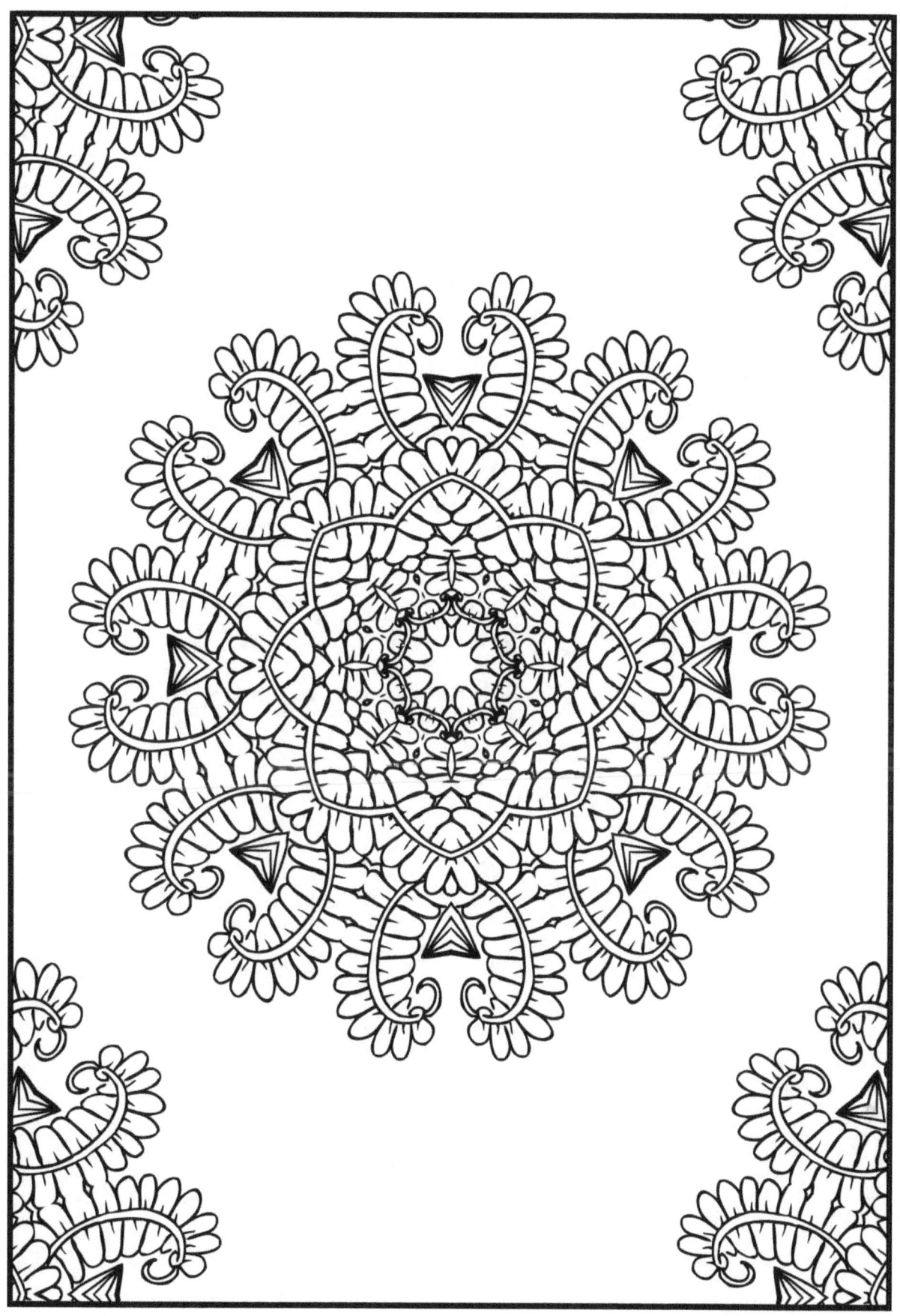

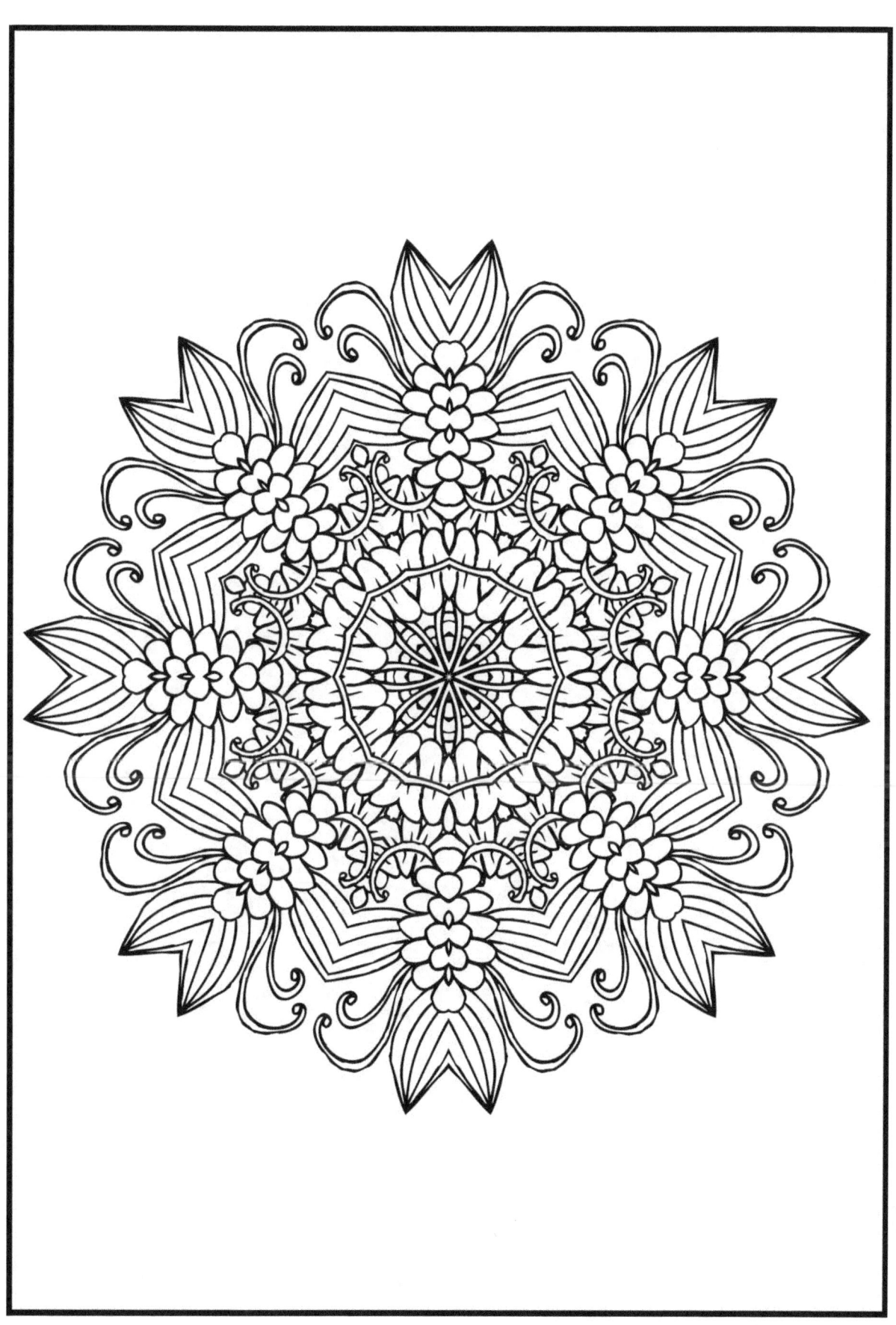

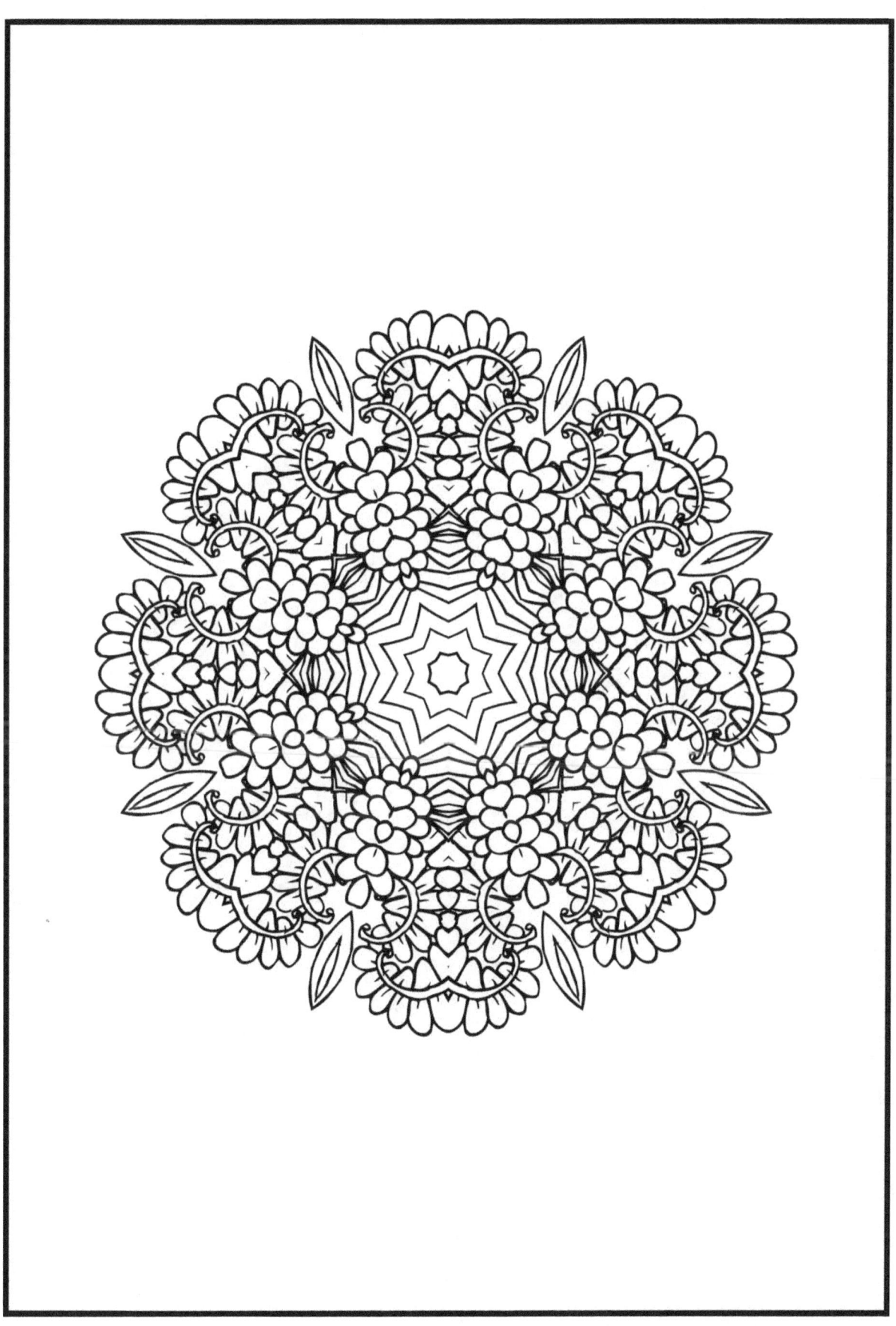

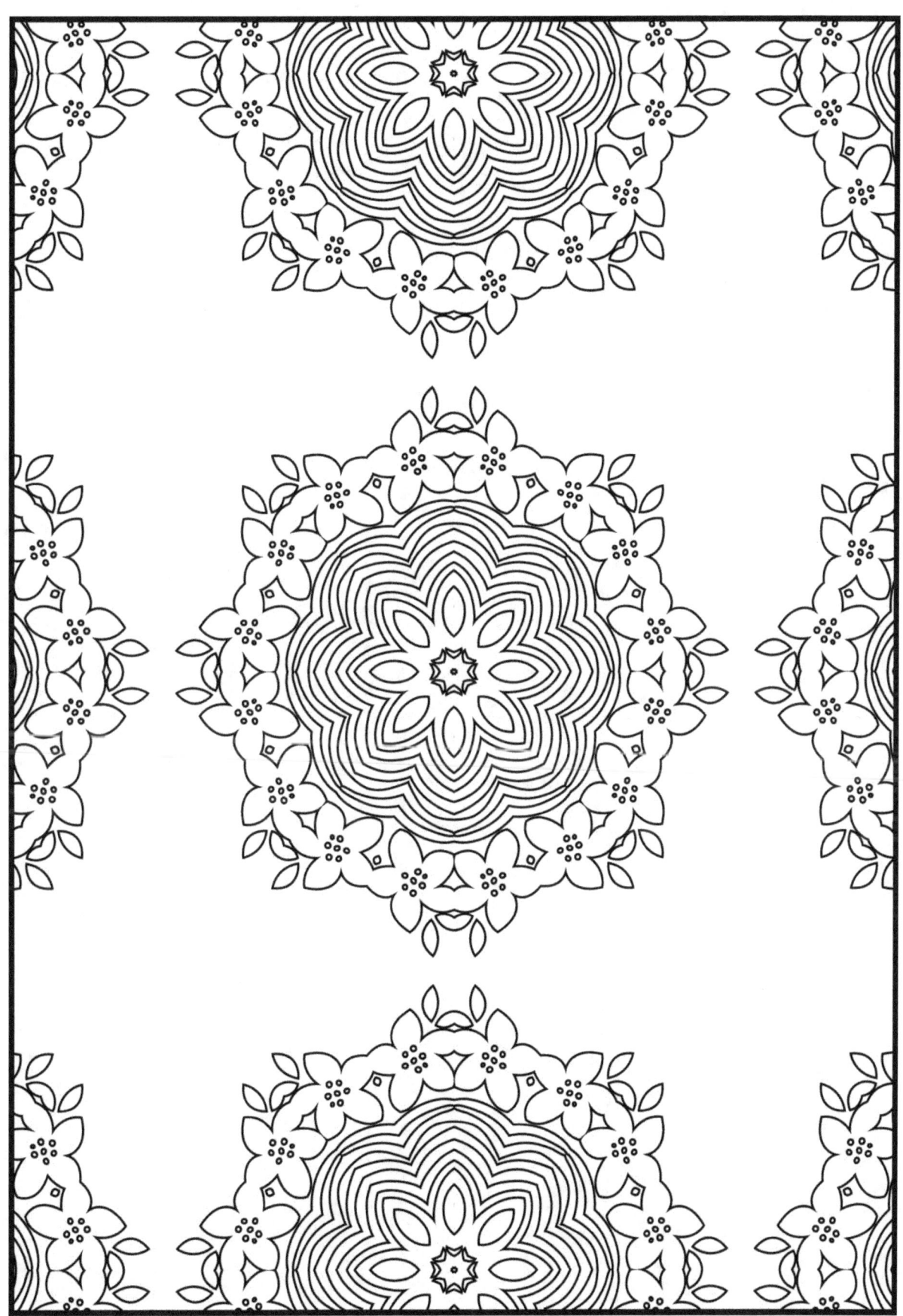

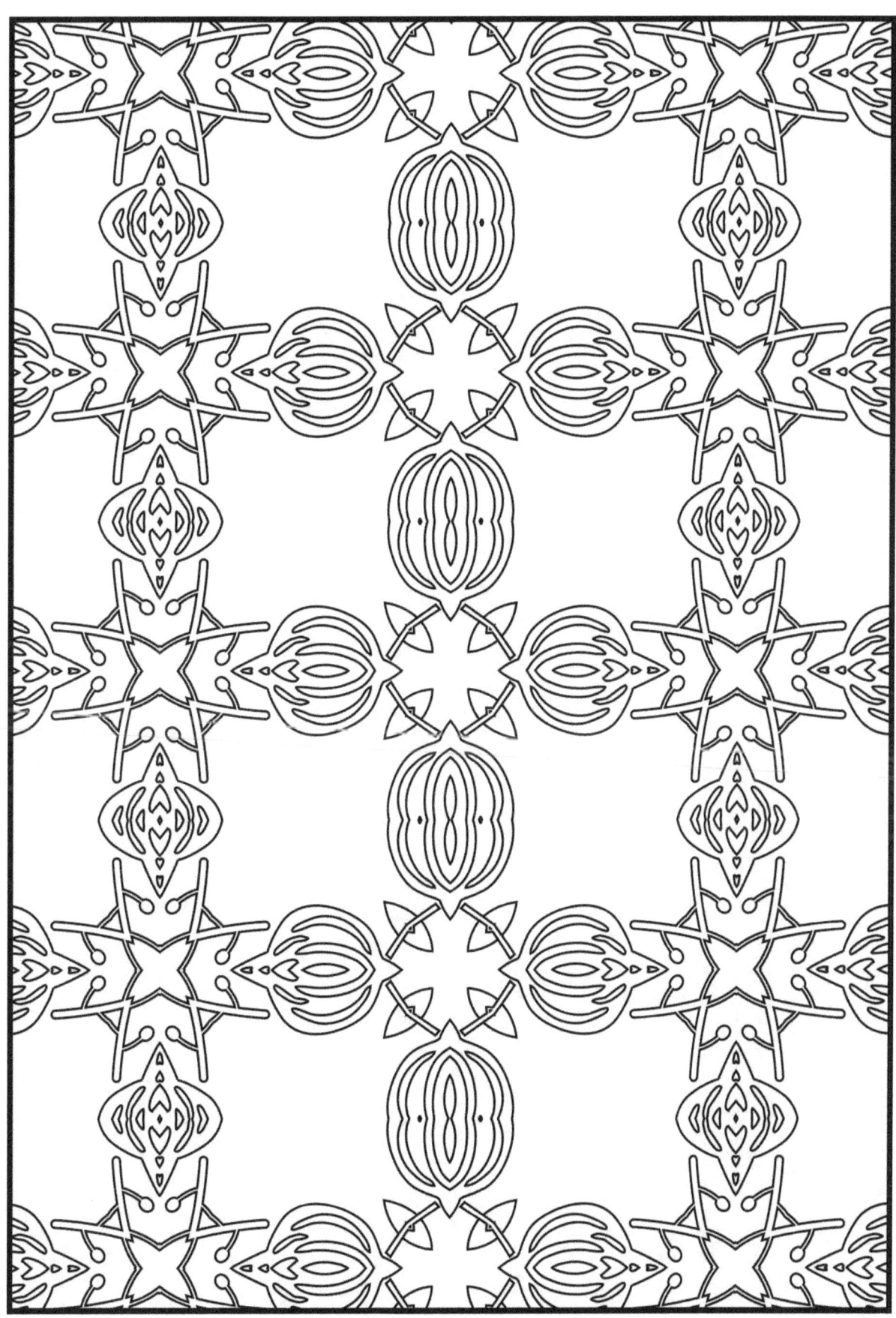

www.ingramcontent.com/pod-product-compliance
Lightning Source LLC
Chambersburg PA
CBHW080542190526
45169CB00007B/2596